QUOTATIONS OF CHAIRMAN MAO
A Short Bibliographical Study

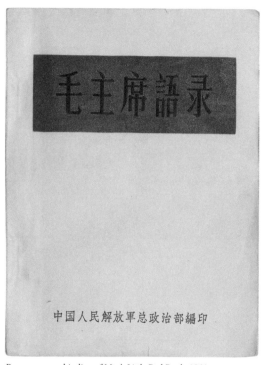

毛主席語录

中国人民解放軍总政治部編印

Paper wrapper binding of Mao's Little Red Book, 1964
First edition with publisher's imprint at the bottom

QUOTATIONS OF CHAIRMAN MAO
1964 – 2014

A short bibliographical study published on the
occasion of the fiftieth anniversary of
Mao's **Little Red Book**

Justin G. Schiller

The Grolier Club • Battledore Ltd
New York • 2014

Published in conjunction with an
exhibition held at The Grolier Club
to commemorate the fiftieth anniversary of
Mao's **Little Red Book**
November 13, 2014 – January 10, 2015
Curated by Justin G. Schiller

Of this monograph 1000 copies printed
Fort Orange Press, Inc., Albany NY

The fonts Minion and Palatino used in this catalogue are
intended to resemble a similar old style serif type used by the
Foreign Languages Press with the first English translation
of *Quotations from Chairman Mao Tse-Tung* (Peking 1966)

ISBN 978-1-60583-056-8

CONTENTS

Sources and Early Printing History

Frontispiece portrait of Chairman Mao
First edition, 1964

*A*pparently unknown to bibliographers, the gradual development in putting together short texts from the published writings and speeches of Chairman Mao Zedong (1893–1976) to eventually create the world-famous **Quotations of Chairman Mao** (*Mao Zhuxi Yulu*) is more complex than originally believed. Sometimes referred to as the "Chinese Bible," it was originally published on a very restricted basis in June or July 1964 (its preface is dated May 1964) and certainly holds a world record for most copies printed of a single work in under four years (720 million copies by the end of 1967, with current estimates today surpassing five billion copies). Its idea was conceived by Lin Biao (1907–71) as a book of inspirational reading and first published for the General Political Department of the People's Liberation Army (PLA). For several years Lin promoted a campaign that everyone should study Chairman Mao's thoughts, and the PLA newspaper printed daily extracts from his selected texts that often formed topics for evening discussion groups. This was an expedient way for soldiers to be indoctrinated with Mao's ideological philosophy, since most of them were not well educated, and brief extracts of easy to understand words could help focus their comprehension and analysis.

Prior to the October 1949 founding of the People's Republic of China (PRC), five editions of Mao Zedong's *Selected Works* had been published in various "Liberated Area" (Communist occupied) locations in China between 1944 and 1948, their texts taken from newspaper articles and oral transcriptions but apparently none sanctioned by their author. These were filled with misprints, errors and omissions, often excluding important articles entirely and including texts by other writers incorrectly attributed to Mao. Thus, the Central Committee of the Chinese Communist Party (CCP) decided a new edition of Mao's *Selected Works* was needed, so following the liberation of Beijing in February 1949, a committee was formed to prepare and organize an authoritative version. The text selections were made in consultation with its author and Mao also agreed to proofread everything and organize additional notes with explanations. It was produced by the People's Publishing House (Beijing) and arranged in chronological sections to coincide with periods of recent Chinese history: the first revolutionary civil war (1924–27) and second revolutionary civil war (1927–37) [Volume One], the war of resistance against Japan (1937–45) [Volumes Two and Three], and the third revolutionary civil war (1945–49) against the Nationalists [Volume Four]. The first volume was printed in October 1951 to coincide with the second anniversary of the founding of the PRC and its additional three parts were published over the next nine years. These became the source from which texts were selected and used to create the Little Red Book, and for that reason we provide bibliographical descriptions (English translations are followed by romanized Chinese in parentheses; measurements are height x width).

Selected Works of Mao Tse-Tung (Mao Zedong Xuanji), Volume One (Di Yi Juan)
Peking, China: People's Publishing House (Beijing, Zhongguo: Renmin Chubanshe), October 1951
Printed by Xinhua Printing Factory, Peking First Branch Factory
Price: 15,000 yuan; 200,000 copies printed, first edition
208 x 151 mm
[i] half-title in red, [iii] title-page in red with a green ink double border, inserted portrait plate of the author captioned (brown ink), i–ii (Introduction), i–vi (Contents Index), 296 pp. + [i] (Colophon)

Selected Works of Mao Tse-Tung (Mao Zedong Xuanji), Volume Two (Di Er Juan)
Peking, China: People's Publishing House (Beijing, Zhongguo: Renmin Chubanshe), March 1952
Printed by Xinhua Printing Factory, Peking First Branch Factory

Price: 25,000 yuan; 500,000 copies printed, first edition
208 x 151 mm
[i] half-title in red, [iii] title-page in red with a green ink double border, [iv] errata notice indicating that the essay "On Contradiction" which is included in this book belongs in Volume One and will be moved in future printings, [x] (Contents Index), (297–)805 pp. + [i] (Colophon)

Selected Works of Mao Tse-Tung (Mao Zedong Xuanji), Volume Three (Di San Juan)
Peking, China: People's Publishing House (Beijing, Zhongguo: Renmin Chubanshe), February 1953
Printed by Xinhua Printing Factory
Price: 15,000 yuan; 500,000 copies printed, first edition, "1-3" code
208 x 151 mm
[i] half-title in red, [iii] title-page in red with a green ink double border, i–iv (Contents Index), (807–)1144 pp. + [i] (Colophon)

Selected Works of Mao Tse-Tung (Mao Zedong Xuanji), Volume Four (Di Si Juan)
Peking, China: People's Publishing House (Beijing, Zhongguo: Renmin Chubanshe), September 1960
Printed by Peking Xinhua Printing Factory
Price: 1.4 yuan; 1,000,000 copies printed, "1001.479" code
208 x 151 mm
[i] half-title in red, [iii] title-page in red with a green ink double border, i–vi (Contents Index), (1121–)1520 pp. + [i] (Colophon), with an additional errata slip inserted (8 lines) explaining that this volume has been repaginated to conform to the latest reprints (i.e., "second edition") of the earlier volumes which have been re-edited and with changed format.

All of the above texts are printed in vertical format (to be read top down), which did not change to a horizontal format (left to right) until 1966.

A fifth book was planned as early as 1960, to include selected writings from 1949-57, during the early PRC period, but Chairman Mao resisted its production as he felt his essays and speeches on Socialist Construction were still evolving compared to those on his Democratic Revolution policies contained in the earlier volumes. More perspective was needed before one could judge the best appropriate texts to join his otherwise sacred writings. But Mao did agree that a committee could begin reviewing his later work, and several fascicles beginning in 1968 survive that were drafts printed "for internal use only" containing a selection of these later essays (not all of which were eventually adopted). Less than a month following Mao's death, his successor Chairman Hua (Guofeng) agreed on the publication of Volume Five, which followed six months later. It included 70 texts by Mao from October 21, 1949 to November 18, 1957, of which 46 articles had never before been printed in any other form. Another change in party leadership the following year considered these additions and concluded they had gone too far to the left as Deng Xiaoping began a shift in emphasis towards economic reform and away from Mao and his Little Red Book. Consequently, in some circles, this fifth volume is discredited and not considered part of the larger work that the first four volumes represent. Nonetheless, its bibliographical description follows:

Selected Works of Mao Tse-Tung (Mao Zedong Xuanji), Volume Five (Di Wu Juan)
Peking, China: People's Publishing House (Beijing, Zhongguo: Renmin Chubanshe), April 1977
Printed by Peking Xinhua Printing Factory
Price: 1.25 yuan; first edition, "1001.1123" code
208 x 151 mm
[i] half-title in red, [iii] title-page in red with a green ink double border, inserted portrait plate of the author captioned (brown ink), i–ii (Introduction), i–viii (Contents Index), 532 pp.

The first English language translation of the *Selected Works*, volumes 1–3, came out in London in appropriate red cloth by Lawrence & Wishart Ltd, 1954–56 (as four volumes); volumes 4 and 5 were first translated into English and published in Beijing by the Foreign Languages Press in 1961 and 1977 respectively.

Earliest Quotations

Prior to the Little Red Book

R ecent scholarship has brought forth a remarkable paperbound anthology that predates anything similar and marks the beginning of our study:

Philosophical Thought Quotations of Mao Zedong (First Draft). Mao Zedong Zhexue Sixiang Yulu
Compiled by the Philosophy Teaching and Research Office of Shaanxi School, Chinese Communist Party
[Xi'an], May 1960
184 x 132 mm
[iv], 316 pp. printed on rough oatmeal paper; printed paper wrappers.

This comprises a collection of quotations by Mao classified into eight subjects: world outlook; objective law; dialectics of materialism; cognition and practice; fundamental contradictions within society; class struggle and proletarian dictatorship; two varieties of contradictions with different natures; and masses, classes, parties and leadership. They are extracted from his best-known essays as well as from *Selected Works* (vols. 1, 2 and 3).

Two years following this publication, the first book solely titled "Quotations of Chairman Mao" appeared, produced on a single side of Japanese-folded paper and given the appearance of having been printed on a mimeograph or stenograph machine. Like its predecessor it is not in any bibliography of Mao's writings and was identified by a bookseller in Chengdu who described it as the original prospectus for creating the now famous 1964 version of Quotations.

毛泽东哲学思想语录

（初　稿）

中共陕西省委党校哲学教研室汇编

1960年5月

Quotations of Chairman Mao (*"Mao Zhuxi Yulu"*)
Issued by the Intelligence Division of Shenyang Air Force Base, April 10, 1962
191 x 132 mm
8vo, [vii], 71 ff. with the final leaf attached to the inside rear cover; paper wrappers with front cover titled and imprinted, bound by two staples along left margin. At the juncture of both ff. 20/21 and 30/31 there is an unnumbered double-page where the recto sheet continues text from the previous page and its attached verso sheet is blank.

The preface states "Someone from our department went to the Air Force Intelligence Office for study and brought back two documents: one is 'Quotations of Chairman Mao,' the other is 'Connotations on Instructions from the Commander in Chief.' We are reprinting them for comrades inside this division as study and work reference. Please Do Not Lend Out."

Then follows a preliminary introduction: "Mao Zedong Thought was created from the collapse of Imperialism and the victory of Socialism as represented by the Chinese Revolution, collectively out of the people's struggle via the application of the universal truth of Marxism-Leninism," signed below by the Enlarged Meeting of the Central Committee of the Chinese Communist Party "Resolution on Strengthening the Army's Political and Ideological Work." A printing error occurs where this text is actually printed recto on the adjoining blank of the preface leaf with verso

毛主席语录

一九六二年四月

blank and then repeated on the recto of the following sheet. Included on verso of the adjoining blank sheet are two quotations in support of Mao's texts, one by Liu Shaoqi:

> It is the duty of every Party member to study Mao Zedong Thought, to spread Mao Zedong Thought, and to let Mao Zedong Thought's directive guide his work.

The other is by Lin Biao:

> One must take the study of Mao Zedong Thought to hand: to grasp its spiritual essence, and to grasp its main method, i.e., materialistic dialectics. One must study diligently and practice a lot; much practice must be interchanged with deep and penetrating study, a lot of application in reality, a lot of linking to reality, do not study the past.

By this time Mao's *Selected Works* in four volumes (1951–1960) had become the chief source of knowledge within China for reading and learning the Chairman's ideas. Images of their gleaming white paper covers lettered in red and gold were constantly reproduced on posters, in newspapers and magazines, underneath glazed ceramics, and as part of porcelain figurines. It was natural that these texts would be used to select excerpts for daily military reading. The person in charge of these selections is recorded as Tian Xiaoguang, an editor at the People's Liberation Army newspaper, though credit for creating such a manual of inspirational readings from Mao's writings and speeches (eventually known as the Little Red Book) has always been given to Lin Biao.

By 1959 Lin had been promoted to defense minister and that put him in control of the People's Liberation Army, incorporating not only land forces and navy but also the air force, which was based in Shenyang. Further research into the origin and printing history of **Quotations of Chairman Mao** (*"Mao Zhuxi Yulu"*) has uncovered several variant specimen prototypes that originate from Shenyang and were mostly printed in 1963 but not officially published. Each variant contains essentially the same text comprising several hundred excerpts by Mao from 1929 through August 1963 divided into five divisions, 16 chapters and 64 sections, collating with a title-page, Lin's short endorsement (see below), 7 pages of index at the front and 351 pages of text. Very few copies were produced of each version from which the final texts were selected for use in the first published edition of 1964. Several copies are dated, some are undated, in each instance with type reset to correct previous errors. None of them include a portrait of Chairman Mao but they all have a brief quote by Lin Biao paraphrasing model hero Lei Feng: *"Everyone should study the Chairman's writings, follow his teachings, act according to his instructions and be Chairman Mao's good soldier,"* here typeset in red ink, afterwards eliminating the final statement about "good soldier" and also in 1964 reproduced on a single inserted leaf following Mao's portrait, copying Lin's own calligraphy.

(1a) **Quotations of Chairman Mao** ("*Mao Zhuxi Yulu*"), subtitled "(For the Use of Brigade Socialist Education), compiled by the Air Force Political Department of Shenyang Military District, August 1963", all printed in red ink, the date crossed out in ink in the one copy located and overwritten "First Printed by the Political Department of the Air Force Party School, September 6th, 1963." An inscription on its title-page indicates *"Approved for copying For Use as Reference"* signed Ye Dong.

12mo, [iv], 24 pp. with an introduction dated August 10th 1963, preceded by an undated version of the main text (iii, 7 pp. index + 351 pp.) with Lin's endorsement in four lines citing its source *"On Resolving to Strengthen the Army's Political and Ideological Work,"* Central Military Commission meeting.

Bound at the end is a second pamphlet without imprint titled "Quotations from Comrade Mao Zedong on Enhancing Vigilance and Strengthening War Preparation" (32 pp.). The three books are uniquely bound together with a hand-lettered title-page at the front citing "The Political Department of the Air Force 011 Brigade." Of the 150 quotations included in the first volume, 127 are from the writings of Mao and 27 from Lin Biao and the Central Military Commission.

毛主席語录

（供連队社会主义教育之用）

沈陽軍区空軍政治部

(1b)

(1b) ***Quotations of Chairman Mao*** (*"Mao Zhuxi Yulu"*).
No imprint but dated October 1963 on the title-page,
Lin's endorsement in three lines of red type, with all
page numerals printed in italics. In this version the
final text of Lin changes *"good soldier"* to now read
"good student."
12mo, [iii], 7 pp. index + 351 pp.; bound in glazed red
boards with front cover stamped with title and five-
pointed star, colored pale yellow/white.

 removed — placing single reference:

(1c)

(1c) ***Quotations of Chairman Mao*** (*"Mao Zhuxi Yulu"*). Shenyang: Compiled and printed by the Political Department, Air Force Division, Shenyang Military Region, December 1963.

12mo, [iii] with Lin's endorsement in four lines identical to that present in 1a; copies have been noted in printed stiff wrappers and also inserted inside blind-stamped red vinyl.

Cited in Guo Dongpeng's bibliography *Outline for Cataloguing Mao Zedong's Works* (Harbin 2006, p. 71), referring to two similar versions of 351 pages, an undated edition without imprint ascribed to 1963 and this dated version.

Undated copies have been noted as bound in red boards stamped in yellow with cover title and small star (see below), others in gilt-stamped red cloth with their spine gilt-titled with double-bar rules at top and bottom (one example with a gilt scroll ornament between the bars). That with the extra scroll ornament has Lin's four-line endorsement in red type as in 1a and 1c title-page verso; the other version has the identical text printed on a separate leaf following the title-page. Neither version identifies the source. An unusual undated version in dark burgundy boards follows 1b with Lin's endorsement in three lines mentioning "good student" and having page numerals in italics. The binding is impressed only on the front cover with title and star in either silver or tarnished white, with a cover imprint that has been crossed out and mutilated.

(1d)

(1d) ***Quotations of Chairman Mao*** (*"Mao Zhuxi Yulu"*).
The final prototype version with 351 pages follows
Lin's endorsement, as in 1a and 1c, identifying its
source, here with title page dated May 1964. Copies
are bound in either printed paper wrappers or tan
linen with the title and star on front cover and title on
spine, all stamped in red. Two states exist: one with
an errata slip comprising six corrections to be made
in the text, the second version with the text errors
corrected. A reference in one copy examined identifies
its distributor as the Political Department of Army
Unit 6573.

To reduce the text to a manageable pocket size format, Ms. Tian, the PLA newspaper editor, prepared her first draft with 23 chapters comprising 200 different entries, revised it to 25 chapters with 267 quotations, and eventually 30 chapters comprising 250 pages when it was finally published by the General Political Department. Although there is no colophon or date on the title-page, its preface is signed May 1964, so traditionally that has always been cited as when this first edition was actually produced, but allowing for printing and binding it may not have been published until the following month. For a variety of reasons that are beyond the scope of this work, **Quotations of Chairman Mao** (*"Mao Zhuxi Yulu"*) became the most identifiable icon of Communist China and its eventual Great Proletarian Cultural Revolution.

At about the same time, a small oblong version with the same title and text printed on the recto of 161pp mimeographed varying colored papers indicates its 150 quotations were assembled from newspapers and magazine between 1963 and April 1964. The editor is identified as Wang Shangwen and the introduction, dated May 1964, is by the 6573 Military Troop. About 120 quotations are from Chairman Mao with the remainder by Lin Biao, Liu Shaoqi, Xiao Hua and other military commissioners.

First Edition
Binding Variants

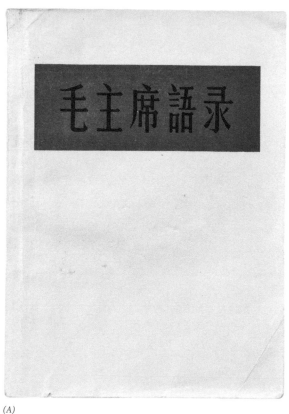

(A)

Paper wrapper binding of Mao's Little Red Book
without printed publisher's imprint at the bottom

*T*he 1964 first published edition has a page size larger than subsequent printings measuring 137 cm. (5 3/8 inches) height and occurs in two completely different bindings: (A) in printed paper wrappers with its title in black within an oblong red rectangular box on upper cover, often with the publisher's name in black at the bottom, red lettered spine and a blank rear cover; and (B) in red vinyl textured plastic incised with the title and a red star below, being a separate protective jacket where stiff plain white cardboard covers are inserted adjacent to a linen-backed spine with sewn head- and tail-bands.

Although the text for both bindings appears to be identical, according to Ms. Tian those in printed paper wrappers were released first while the red vinyl plastic covers were still being designed/manufactured, as its copies required a sturdier binding support. These followed a short time thereafter: the printed wrappers were intended for individual high-ranking officers while the red vinyl covers were for use by brigade teams of up to eight men. By the start of the Cultural Revolution (August 1966), the red vinyl covers had become preferred for symbolizing Mao's slogan "The East is Red" and the more fragile paper wrappers were no longer produced.

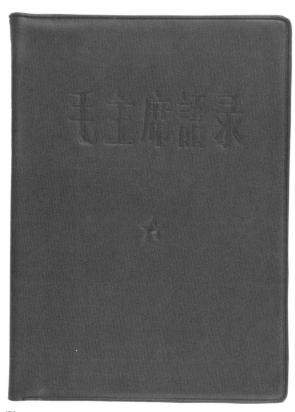

(B)
Red vinyl binding of Mao's Little Red Book

There exist at least three variant vinyl trial bindings, each comprising the 1964 first issue in printed paper wrappers loosely laid inside flexible plastic: (1) of blue-green vinyl with the fourth and fifth Chinese characters forming "Yulu," meaning "Quotations," on the incised front jacket printed in simplified form rather than normal Chinese characters, and without any five-

(1)

pointed star; (2) in light blue vinyl with the front cover lettered in script, also without any star; and (3) of dark blue vinyl with the title text character corrected and having an oversized five pointed star. The blue color is customary in China for use with trial bindings, and all three probably predate the corrected red vinyl covers usually associated with this book.

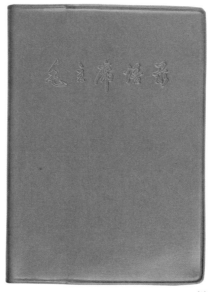

(2)

**First Edition
Textual Variants**

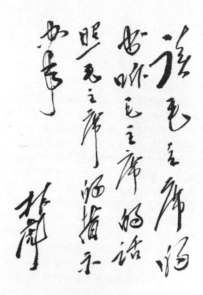

Lin Biao calligraphic endorsement leaf with
superfluous mark; see corrected version opposite

*I*t is generally accepted that all copies comprising only thirty chapters and with texts ending at page 250 are first editions. The absence of publishing data is because this was not considered an official book when it was simultaneously produced at different locations in China from stereotyped plates, thus making local distribution easier. As head of national defense Lin Biao was invited to write an endorsement, and Lin chose three sentences from the diary of the revolutionary model hero Lei Feng: *"Study Chair-*

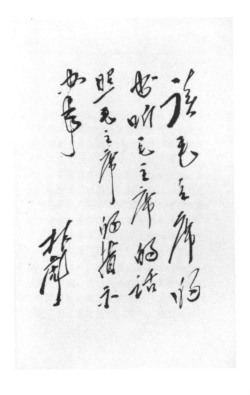

man Mao's writings, follow his teachings and act according to his instructions." He wrote them out in a calligraphic script but made a mistake with one word: a superfluous brush stroke occurring in the second vertical line from the right, second character from the top (*ting*), which means "listen to" or "obey," thus giving it the English equivalent of crossing a "t" or dotting an "i" twice. This error was discovered only after the book had been printed, and new plates were eventually made but they were apparently not used until the third edition of August 1965.

Lin had been part of the Red Army since joining Mao's forces in 1928, and gradually became a top-ranking leader: in 1959 he was appointed defense minister, second only to Mao in the military hierarchy. His promotion of the Little Red Book added significant influence to his profile, so by 1967 he was designated vice-chairman, and at the Ninth Congress (1969) it was confirmed that he would be Mao's heir and successor. Jealous factions whispered rumors that Lin and his family were plotting to assassinate Mao and gain early control of the Chinese Communist Party (CCP). While never totally proven, it caused Lin, his wife Ye Qun and their son to suddenly leave on a military transport for an undisclosed destination, when their plane was shot down over Mongolia on the evening of September 12, 1971. When this news was finally released to the Chinese people after more than a year, it came with a proclamation that Mao's close comrade-in-arms for nearly a half-century had disgraced himself and his name was to be eradicated from modern history. Consequently, his endorsement leaf in all copies of the Little Red Book and elsewhere were to be torn out or otherwise defaced as a sign of loyalty to Mao and the CCP. Indeed, not removing it could easily be a liability. Therefore, many surviving copies in the Chinese language have that page legitimately torn away, mutilated or censored following this decree.

Of the earliest printed text issued by the General Political Department of the Chinese People's Liberation Army there are three variants with no known priority firmly established as to their distribution, but it is believed that copies with the text error on pages 82/3 represent the earliest printed version:

(1) Some copies in red vinyl binding (including those from the Central Advanced Party School Library of the CCP) contain a text error at the bottom of page 82 and top of 83, with a printed erratum slip: "*In this book between pages 82 and 83, because of a printing error, please read 'li yong wo men' instead of 'li men wo yong.'*" In these copies the Lin endorsement is printed in brown ink, but no copies in printed paper wrappers have been identified with this error uncorrected.

勘　　误
本书 82 页转 83 页之间，由于印刷错误，将"利用我们"错为"利们我用"。特此更正。

勘　　误
本书 82 页转 83 页之间，由于印刷错误，将"利用我们"错为"利们我用"。特此更正。

Two versions of printed erratum slip

(2) Other copies in red vinyl binding have text pages 82/3 correctly printed and are known with the Lin endorsement with the error in either brown or black ink.

(3) All copies examined in printed paper wrappers have corrected text at pages 82/3 and the Lin endorsement with the error printed only in black ink.

Even within the above groups one may find variations in the quality and thickness of the paper used, apparently due to the use of stereotype plates in different printing centers throughout the country. In one instance the portrait frontispiece of Chairman Mao changes to a light brown color halftone (again, without known priority).

The first four leaves for all three versions are separately printed from the rest of the book and comprise a half-title printed in red ink *"Workers of the World, Unite!"*; a title-page with the title and central star printed in red while the publisher's imprint below and a double-ruled border around the entire page are printed in green; a finely delineated portrait of Chairman Mao (usually found with a tissue guard) printed in brown; and the facsimile calligraphic endorsement by Lin Biao (always with its printing error) printed in either brown or black ink. This is followed by all-black-ink letterpress text: (1/2) an introduction signed by the General Political Department dated 1st May 1964; (1/2) Table of Contents listing thirty chapters; and then paginated 1–250 with Chairman Mao's text.

質　量　检　查　证

毛　主　席　語　录		
质　量　检　查　员	1	号
出　　厂	1 9 6 4 年 8 月	

此书如印刷、裝訂质量有問
題。請随书将此証一起寄本厂
　地址：沈阳市 和平区 三
　　　好街一段三号
　沈阳軍区印刷厂技术科收
　（請将寄回地点写淸）

A quality control slip has been found inside a few copies of these books dated August 1964 asking the reader:

If there is any problem with printing or binding of this book, please send this book along with this certificate to the following address:

Address: No. 3, San Hao Street, He Ping District Shengyang City (Liaoning Province)

The Technical Department of the Printing Factory of Shenyang Military District

　(Please write this address clearly and carefully)

There are two additional versions that exist which also are considered "first editions" in China, both still conforming to 30 chapters of text and most likely issued either at the same time or soon after:

毛主席語录

★

中国人民解放軍总政治部編印
中共四川省委工交政治部翻印

(4) Identical in format and content to no. 3 but having a double-line imprint on both the printed front wrapper and the title-page: "The General Political Department of the Chinese People's Liberation Army, The Ministry of Metallurgical Industry."

(5a) Smaller format with page height 125 cm (4 7/8 inches), which afterwards became the standard size for all subsequent printings of the Little Red Book. Copies are only known in printed wrappers (following the same design as on the larger-sized version) but issued without the four inserted colored-ink preliminaries, thus beginning directly with a Preface [1/2], Table of Contents [1/2], and then paginated 1–252 with Chairman Mao's text, here slightly expanded due to the reduced page size. It has been suggested that this version must also be considered a first printing (like nos. 1–3) but without the color-printed stereotype plates which had been accidentally omitted when shipped to some regional printers (where this was printed we do not know). However, these text pages required *new* printing plates because the text area itself got slightly reduced when the format became smaller, so this argument is not wholly convincing.

(5b) Identical to no. 5a is a similar version having a double-line imprint on the front cover (most likely produced at the same time) adding that it was made for the "Political Department of the Railway Corps of the People's Liberation Army" (still with no printing location identified). Because the contents of both these issues comprise the original 30 text chapters, it is certainly very early in this book's history and is itself quite a rare variant.

In order to meet the initial demand for studying Mao's works by army officials and soldiers, the editors produced an abridged version of the Little Red Book compiled by the Air Force Political Department of the Shenyang Military Region, reorganizing the order of the quotations and adding some new ones, while cutting out others:

Quotations of Chairman Mao (*"Mao Zhuxi Yulu"*). [Beijing:] Printed for Army Unit 4118 of the Chinese People's Liberation Army, June 1964. 16mo, [i] preface + 142 pp.; printed brown paper wrappers with its title and date printed in red ink on the front cover.

There is a large paper version (7-3/8 x 5-1/4 inches) of the 1964 first edition, collating as usual with only 30 chapters, including the error in Lin's calligraphic endorsement, [4]ff., 2, 2, 209pp. for distribution within the Inner Mongolian Autonomous Region.

A two-volume work having the same title *Mao Zhuxi Yulu* was also issued in a loose-leaf binding with shoe-lace ties compiled by the Workers' Daily Newspaper Editorial Department, October 1964, listing Chairman Mao's quotations by different topics limited to only 20 chapters.

(a)

There have been variations found in the official portraits used as frontispiece of the Little Red Book. The first four editions used the images shown here a) June 1964, 1st edition; b) March and August 1965, 2nd and 3rd editions respectively; and c) November 1965, 4th edition, which used a much earlier portrait of Chairman Mao. Later editions, reprints and translations all reverted to the original portrait from the 1964 first edition.

(b)

(c)

Second and Third Editions

毛主席語录

中共黑龙江省委《党的生活》編輯部編

黑龙江人民出版社出版

一九六五年

Title-page of the 2nd edition, March 1965
containing 32 chapters and collating 260 pages

*I*t has been recently stated by Daniel Leese in a collection of essays in *Mao's Little Red Book,* edited by Alexander C. Cook (Cambridge University Press, 2014), that the original print run of the 1964 first edition of Quotations was 4.2 million copies. He also indicates that by August 1965 this had tripled to over 12 million copies due to demand. This was largely due to the production of stereotyped plates used in several different locations simultaneously. These plates were used to produce a second edition (March 1965) that was printed in Northeast China at Harbin by the Heilongjiang Province People's Publishing House. This new edition added two more chapters of text and changed the portrait image of Mao. Curiously, of five copies located for examination, four in printed paper wrappers and one in red stamped boards, they all appear never to have had Lin's endorsement; there is also no preface included and Mao's text is expanded to 260 pages (now with 32 chapters).

The first complete edition of Mao's Quotations is the third edition, upon which all subsequent versions and translations are based. This was published in August 1965 and adds a 33rd chapter, reverting back to a slightly smaller-size image of Mao's original portrait as first printed in 1964 and now expanding the text to 270 pages. As with the earliest printings it is published for the General Political Department with a similar title-page and imprint as in the 1964 first edition and intended only "for internal circulation." Copies appear in both printed paper wrappers and red vinyl plastic. For unknown reasons a few copies are known with the Lin endorsement in its uncorrected earlier state (from 1964). There also occurs (rarely) a seven-line errata slip changing the citation on page 244 but not mentioning another alteration at page 208. Most copies, however, have the Lin endorsement leaf in its corrected form.

Copies of this third edition sometimes have extra material pasted inside, such as *"Latest Instructions"* printed in red ink with more Mao quotations, and also small pamphlets like *When You Meet Problems or Questions, You Can Find The Answers in Chairman Mao's Quotations* which may list up to 100 difficulties found in daily life (cross-referenced to Mao's *Selected Works*). This may be followed by a list of topics for discussion groups dealing with Mao's thoughts, issued by the Beijing Dongfeng Printing Factory. Thereafter, many more editions of Mao were printed locally, sometimes several printings within the same month but from different cities, occasionally making changes such as using an earlier Mao portrait as frontispiece, as was done by the Jilin Province People's Publishing House (November 1965). This version is otherwise identical to the August 1965 complete version comprising 270 pages in 33 chapters. In August 1966, a large print edition of Quotations was produced that followed the text and order of the August 1965 complete version.

Finally, in December 1965, a special Quotations was produced for the cadre leadership to check the actual quotations against their original sources. It is marked "For Internal Use, not for circulation" and was published in Hubei by the People's Publishing House, collating with three inserted leaves: the usual half-title printed verso of the front free endpaper, the title-page, and Mao's portrait. It is possible Lin's endorsement was included but in the one copy located, it is no longer intact. Following the portrait is a letterpress introduction dated November 1965 with three pages of contents listing 36 chapters, followed by 458 paginated text pages plus a colophon. this is all bound in stiff white cloth stamped in red characters on both the front cover and spine.

毛主席語录

中国人民解放軍总政治部編印

Title-page of the 3rd edition, August 1965
containing 33 chapters and collating 270 pages

Translations

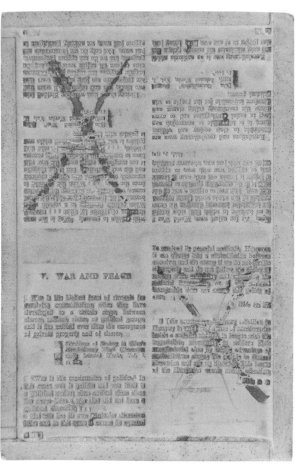

Stereotype printing plate for English text, 1966

A new introduction for the Little Red Book appeared in newspapers on December 16, 1966 and was subsequently added to all future printings of the book (now designated "Second Edition"), and likewise also circulated as a small bifolium for anyone to put inside their older copies. This "Foreword" is signed by Lin Biao and explains how Marxism-Leninism-Mao Thought is "a powerful ideological weapon" for opposing imperialism, revisionism and dogmatism, an inexhaustible source of strength and spiritual guidance for the masses. A few months earlier also signaled the start of a major translation and publication project when the Little Red Book was issued in over 50 different languages of countries where Socialism might triumph. Second editions of many languages were redone in 1972 to remove the endorsements of Lin following disclosures that he was plotting to assassinate Chairman Mao to advance his own leadership.

In an exhibition catalogue for the Humanities Research Center, University of Texas at Austin (1976), Professor William B. Todd described copies of *Mao Zhuxi Yulu* published through September 1966 as being printed "For Internal Circulation Only", *i.e.*, restricted government distribution. However, this changed in October when the East Is Red Publishing House (Beijing) produced the first copies for general sale as well as the first bilingual edition (Chinese-English) ten months later (August 1967).   There was also a second version of Quotations titled *Highest Instructions* (Beijing 1968), which has Mao's quotations arranged alphabetically in Pinyin but with Chinese characters on the left page facing English texts on the right. As for translations into other languages, they were created, printed and distributed chiefly by the government's Foreign Languages Press between 1966 and 1972 with the following versions recorded: Albanian, Arabic, Bengali, Chinese Braille, Bulgarian, Burmese, Cambodian, Czech, Danish, Dutch, English,

Esperanto, Flemish, French, German, Greek, Hausa, Hindi, Hungarian, Icelandic, Indonesian, Italian, Japanese, Kazak, Korean, Laotian, Mongolian, Nepali, Norwegian, Pakistani, Pashto, Persian, Polish, Portuguese, Rumanian, Russian, Serbian. Sinhalese, Spanish, Swahili, Swedish, Tagalog [Filipino], Tamil, Thai, Tibetan, Todo Mongolian, Turkish, Urdu, Uygur and Vietnamese. In addition, there were four versions printed in Israel: a pirated English-language reprint (title-page in black ink) containing a 1966 Hebrew colophon and then three 1967 Hebrew versions, each a new translation by different publishers. In January 1968, two unauthorized Chinese versions were produced in Hong Kong: a photomechanical miniature (271 pp., 2-7/8 x 2 inches) by the Zhonghua Book Printing Factory, January 1968, and a set of 112 double-sided note cards with quotations contained inside a red plastic case with folding opaque lid. Several Chinese printings were also produced in raised Braille letters during the 1960s, including one version actually bound in an extra-large red vinyl plastic cover with Mao's portrait following the original style. And the Foreign Languages Press also issued a series of *Quotations From Chairman Mao Tse-Tung Set To Music* (1968) as 20 separate cards (mostly bifolium) including a "Key to Chinese Phonetic Symbols" which would aid in the reading of the Pinyin transcription of the lyrics.

The first English version printed in the United States appeared in March 1967 in bright red wrappers as a Bantam paperback, edited by Stuart R. Schram with an introduction by A. Doak Barnett. And in 1968 CMS Records (New York) issued their album no. 105 of "Direct QUOTATIONS from the 'LITTLE RED BOOK' selected by Trevor Reese" and read by Shakespearean actor Martin Donegan.

The Little Red Book continued to be printed in huge quantities for mass distribution up until the time of

Mao's death on September 9, 1976. Earlier that year there was produced a 10th anniversary version of the Quotations, newly excerpted from publications between May 1966–May 1976 with the notation "For Internal Study Only." The text is entirely different, compiled with excerpts from Mao's talks and writings during the past ten years to repudiate Deng and oppose the rehabilitation of right-leaning elements. A demonstration at Tiananmen Square on April 5, 1976 to memorialize the death of Zhou Enlai (January 8, 1976), was turned into a criticism of Deng Xiaoping by the Gang of Four. Following Zhou's death, Deng was appointed vice-premier.

But Mao's death brought a symbolic end to the Cultural Revolution (which had used the Little Red Book as a frequent symbol representing his authority) and by the late 1970s a change in government discouraged its further circulation. Millions upon millions of copies were collected and destroyed as waste paper even while the cult of Maoism continued. It was during the centenary of Mao Zedong's birth (1993) that copies were once again printed, this time as facsimiles in English, French and German, being exact replicas dated 1966 as in the original and with "First Edition" printed behind each title-page. Copies can easily be distinguished by their bright shiny red laminated covers and often the presence of colored photograph portraits near the front. As they can still be found all over China, it's most likely there continues to be recent reprints.

No one can deny that Mao is the father of his country, truly a symbol of power and reverence who has been exonerated for the mistakes of his reign and consequently recognized for his achievements as hope for China's future. His Little Red Book forms a brilliant compilation that is still readable and admired today for its political theories and strategies.

ACKNOWLEDGEMENTS

*T*his monograph is based upon personal inspection during over a decade of researching the printing history of the Little Red Book, as well as from interviewing senior specialists at the National Library (Beijing), and information gathered from various private collectors, librarians and dealers throughout the People's Republic of China: Dong Zhongchao, Gao Shangheng, Hao Yu, Li Fan, Liu Yuejin, Liu Zhanquan, Lu Pengxiang, Shi Jinyan, Tian Xiaoguang, Qing Wang, Yan Huizeng, Zhang Weishu and Zhao Hong. My thanks go to Oliver Lei Han for working together on an earlier draft published in the *Antiquarian Book Review* (London, November 2003) and expanded for BibSite, the online resource of the Bibliographical Society of America; also to Don Cohn, Greg Gillert and George Ong for help in editing this study and to Eric Holzenberg of The Grolier Club for encouraging this publication. The English language translations from the Chinese have been graciously provided by Dr. Stefan Landsberger, who likewise reviewed this text several times, for which I am especially grateful. The photography is by Luke Carquillat with the assistance of Dennis M. V. David, who also organized the final layout design.

J.G.S.

Endpapers: "Long Live the Success of the January Revolutionary Storm"
Jacquard textile commemorating the Shanghai upheaval, 6 January 1967